Life With God

FIRST STEPS

Curtis Byers

with
Helen Johns

Evangel Publishing House

Nappanee, Indiana 46550

Cover photograph: Jupiterimages Corporation © 2006

Cover design: Matthew Gable

Library of Congress Catalog Card Number: 96-85027

ISBN-10: 0-916035-67-0

ISBN-13: 978-0-916035-67-9

Printed in the United States of America

10 9 8 7 6 5 4 3 2

Contents

Introduction

Scott and Kathy were an attractive couple in their mid-thirties. Scott was from rural Kentucky. His father died when he was twelve, and his mother had raised seven children with little affection. Scott moved to Lexington, and became a cultured and literate man, and a workaholic. Though still insecure, he managed to find a social niche among young professionals.

Kathy was a stay-at-home mother of three young children. She also was highly intelligent, but with a high school education. Scott worked long hours and studied for the college degree that seemed to be the only barrier to the higher reaches of bank administration. Meanwhile, Kathy felt frustrated and trapped.

One night Kathy couldn't take it anymore and visited a married couple, two of her best friends, to tell them she was leaving Scott. She'd had enough unhappiness. Her visit stretched into five hours of deep discussion. Al and Barbara told Kathy that they could teach her techniques which could improve her marriage, perhaps dramatically. But there was another way, they told her, involving far more significant changes, which would get to the root of their problems. It would mean getting to know the God who created intimacy.

Kathy was fascinated, and ready for change. She had never heard God talked about this way before. Finally Kathy said, "For the first time I understand what true intimacy is. I also know that I have never experienced it, my husband never has, and I'm not sure anyone in either of our families has."

Suppose someone approached you and claimed, as Al and Barbara did with Kathy, to have the secret to true and lasting contentment? You've heard that promise on TV, in self-help seminars, from religion, even from gurus on city street corners. You may think, *Oh, sure, I have a pot of gold buried in my back yard, too.*

Many people, perhaps even you, are cynical and hurt by the world and its evil. Relationships often don't last, bringing us pain, or are difficult at best. Many of us realize that we unwittingly hurt others simply by who we are and what we do. It is tempting to withdraw and not risk being close to people anymore. Or we seek short-term help from pop psychology and other quick fixes. We can go take cooking lessons, or driving lessons—lessons of many kinds. But where do we go for joy lessons? Love and contentment must surely be waiting for us somewhere. But how? And with whom?

Most of us have seen enough glimpses of healthy, intimate relationships to suspect that within them lies the essential ingredient for real happiness. Think back on your life. Would you agree that your greatest moments were those spent loving someone—a parent, a sibling, a friend, a spouse—or being loved? In our most private, honest moments, wouldn't we admit that we yearn for better, deeper relationships as a source of happiness?

As you read this book, you will find that it makes a bold claim. It will offer you an almost unbelievable opportunity: to enter into an intimate relationship with someone who will *never* leave, disappoint, or fail you. As you interact, this person will "rub off" on you. He actually claims to *be* love—never fickle, selfish, mean, or unforgiving. When most people interact with this person, they begin to desire to be just like him.

What's more, we will introduce you to a free training manual which shows how this relationship will improve the way you get along with others in your life. You will learn to act in your own best interest, and in the best interest of those around you. Following this manual can be the most challenging, productive, and exciting undertaking imaginable.

If you haven't guessed already, the person is God, and the manual is the Bible—the story of real people who learned to have personal relationships with God. We will discover that, at a point in history, the God of the universe, the maker of everything, chose to become a human being named Jesus. From knowing Jesus and seeing him interact with others, we can learn what it means to have successful relationships—to love and be loved.

Plan to talk about the ideas in this booklet with a friend as you read the Bible together. Think about several questions: Will you acknowledge God and desire to be in relationship with him? Will you welcome into your life the God who loves you—you!—so very much? If so, will you allow this relationship to influence who you are, and who you can become?

The night that Kathy prayed, she asked God into an intimate relationship with her. She not only went back home dedicated to making her marriage work, but determined that her family would be the first in either of their families' histories to achieve real intimacy. Thus, Kathy began the reversal of deeply imbedded patterns, and the restoration of her family to health and wholeness.

Eventually, both Kathy and Scott became open to talking about the spiritual part of their lives. Al and Barbara offered them many helpful insights about how to have a more intimate marriage. However, they shared something of far greater value, the opportunity to get to know God, the originator of intimacy.

Al and Barbara were Christians. Knowing God had given them the courage to face barriers to intimacy in their own marriage. Over time, Kathy and Scott learned that God's love could be a resource to learn how to love each other. God also began to make changes in them that actually made them more loveable. Change in their marriage began with change, by God's help and power, in themselves.

1

The intimacy factor

Marla was a successful young person. The high school year-book was filled with her pictures. Her talents were numerous, and she got along with almost everyone at school. Love and service were the watchwords of her religion and culture. She was rewarded often with gratitude and praise.

Yet Marla's home life had been somber. Each member of her family went off in a different direction, achieving his or her personal goals. Family interaction was rare, with little laughter, communication, or trust.

By the time Marla had moved away from home and established herself in a job, she determined that life in her own family would be different someday. She would make motherhood a priority, spending lots of time with her children. Insofar as it was up to her, she would create the perfect home.

Marla's expectations were not lost on any man she dated. However, her high ideals were not matched by the quality of her interpersonal skills. By her forties, loneliness turned into despair. Marla began looking for love in one-night stands. She sought power in her job, alienating her coworkers. Alcohol became a steady companion, drowning her disappointment in a sea of confusion. Her dreams of family harmony become a lonely, living nightmare.

We live in a world of isolated people, some of them like Marla, and some who do a better job than Marla of masking their loneliness. We pick up the telephone and a machine talks to us instead of a person. We can drive home from work, push the button on our garage door opener, and never have to greet our neighbor. More and more people live in the disappointment and isolation of divorce. All you have to do is watch television sitcoms, daytime soaps, or movies to see that the predominant theme of life these days is the search for intimacy and happiness.

What is the cure for loneliness and isolation? This book will suggest that intimacy is the answer. But what exactly is intimacy? How is it achieved? Does it have counterfeits? These are important questions for our times. Let's search for a definition of intimacy by examining three concepts: truth, love, and trust.

> *True intimacy happens when two wills with similar character and goals align in an atmosphere of total truth.*

Truth. Total honesty in a relationship leads to a tremendous feeling of joy and freedom. Have you ever known someone with whom you could share your wildest dreams without dreading ridicule, or your most shameful secrets without fearing rejection? We can be childlike and playful—happy—in the company of those with whom we share the greatest intimacy. On the positive side, true intimacy happens when two wills with similar character and goals align in an atmosphere of total truth.

Yet there is a negative side to the truth coin: An intimate relationship means that at some point, if we are totally honest and open, we will divulge our weaknesses. Therefore, maintaining total honesty in a relationship means risking being hurt because the other person may use their knowledge against us. When others know our faults, we are open to the pain of betrayal. Remaining in a relationship for very long often means being willing to be hurt, yet sticking with it.

Love. If you have ever lost a good friend, you can confirm that developing intimacy is risky business. People are not perfect. Sometimes we think we are doing our best, yet the relationship sours. We may offer intimacy to a person who cannot or does not know how to return it. Often we blame a malfunctioning relationship on the other person, and fail to see how we are contributing to the increased strain.

What we need to understand is that relationships which fall apart usually do so because of a failure to love. And the reason we fail to love is that we don't have an accurate picture of what real love can be. The kind of love that keeps relationships intact is not a warm or erotic feeling, but is active, unselfish caring.

In fact, the best model for love is not romance but parenting. Healthy love by a parent is an aggressive pursuit of the best interests of a child, even when it is inconvenient, or even when the child is resisting that love. In situations of danger many parents instinctively would give their lives for their children. It is this kind of other-centered, sacrificial love that is the basis for truly intimate relationships. It is the lack of this kind of love in our world which often causes intimacy to degenerate into brokenness.

Trust. The third concept is trust. Trust allows us to surrender our choices to another person. It means not always insisting on our own way. We have confidence in the other person's knowledge, wisdom, and experience. Again, the purest example of what trust means is seen in the relation-

The kind of love that keeps relationships intact is not a warm or erotic feeling, but active, unselfish caring.

ship between a parent and a son or daughter. It is expressed in the loving wisdom of the parents coupled with trust by the child. Obedience makes it possible for parents to teach children about boundaries which create safety. Children who respect loving parents understand that authority and structure can bring them benefits well beyond the harmonious relationship with their parents.

At a basic level, trust is confidence that the other person will not ask us to do something that violates our own conscience or that is bad for us. At a deeper level, trust is confidence that our interests are at least as high a priority for the other person as his or her own. At the highest level, trust, combined with love and truth, creates intimacy. In a truly intimate relationship we are so trusting of the other person's commitment to our well-being that we willingly invite the other to cross over into our most personal thoughts and experiences. We even allow them to help us make crucial decisions, and then count on them to support us no matter what the consequences.

Our most important relationships cannot survive without some degree of intimacy. Indeed, relationships thrive as we put into practice these concepts of love, truth, and trust.

Intimacy with God

Because human beings fail to practice perfect truth, love, and trust, we all experience pain. But what about intimacy with God? If we can really become close to God, and if we open ourselves to intimacy with God, can we be assured that our openness will never be rejected or abused? In other words, can we trust God any more than we can any other person?

The wonderful truth is that, unlike imperfect humans, God simply is not capable of betrayal and relational failure because he is, in his very nature, perfect truth, love, and trust. God cannot lie. He loves us with unending, unfailing love. We can trust him because our well-being is of primary concern to God. He is our parent, our creator, and therefore wishes to constantly care for us as we learn to grow into an obedient, close relationship with him.

These are significant claims, so it is reasonable to ask: How can I know they are true? The answer lies in the person of God, in God's essential, eternal character. We can learn about God's nature in a variety of ways and places, one of them being the Bible.

God of truth. Over the course of hundreds of years God inspired a group of writers. Their collective works became the Bible—the true story of how people have entered into relationships with one another and with God. The Bible is not a collection of rules and consequences. It is the thoughts— the very mind—of God captured on paper. God did not want to be distant, but revealed to us all we need to know about himself and about life. Within the Bible we discover that God cares about truth so much that he gave humanity fundamental, unchanging words which, if acted upon, can become the basis for successful living.

The truth of the Bible is the often-ignored key to human happiness. As we explore the stories of the Bible, we find that God simply is not capable of betrayal. The characters in these stories risk relationships with God through every conceivable circumstance. The stories are about harlots and queens, children and old people, judges and thieves, priests and pagans, laborers and kings. God never betrays them, lies to them, or ceases to care for them. It is through identifying with their experiences that we can begin to believe that God will do the same for us.

God of love. God's unchanging love is available to us one-on-one. The Bible clearly says that you and I can experience direct personal contact with the living God. This good news also means that God wants to offer us a new kind of family within which to be loved and practice new ways of loving other people. This new family consists of people who are being changed by their own relationships with God. Not yet perfect, they too are learning how to be unselfish and fearless in exploring the challenge of offering and receiving intimacy.

God of trust. Finally, having a relationship with God means choosing to allow God to put limits on our behavior. We do so because we completely believe that God has our best interests at heart and has the power to work every circumstance for our ultimate benefit. This kind of trust grows with experience and is called faith. It is a belief of our mind and a trust from our heart, and influences all of our behavior. God will never fail to care for us when we remain in a loving, respectful, obedient relationship with him. God is perfectly trustworthy.

Learning to love the God who is love means choosing truth and trust. Gaining intimacy with God means rejecting false forms of intimacy—sexual promiscuity, or lust for power, fame, and wealth—which we sometimes imagine can help dull the pain of loneliness. Loving God can, for a while, mean living with a greater sense of emptiness because we give up artificial substitutes for intimacy. But soon we begin to realize how far from intimate many of our relationships have been. The person who truly learns to offer intimacy needs never lack it from God, and eventually finds fullness and happiness. What's more, those of us who are starving for lack of intimacy can find ourselves sharing love generously with those around us who need it.

Marla's story could have been different. Had her family of origin practiced a less self-absorbed and a more risk-taking kind of living, Marla might have learned the essentials of truth, love, and trust. Had they learned together about God's concept of intimacy from the Bible, they might have opened themselves to and been able to share it among themselves.

Marla needed a balance of relationship and work. She needed to turn to God for companionship, not to destructive relationships, power, and alcohol. Her desperate search for a happy family could have reached fulfillment in the arms of a loving God.

The rest of this book will look at God's plan for our world, and for restoring humanity to the better relationships we were created to enjoy.

Talk It Over

1. Talk about your own family relationships. What about them was good? What about them would you change if you could relive them?

2. Have you ever experienced lack of truth in a relationship? What happened?

3. Have you ever sought to express love only to find that the other person was incapable of returning love? Has your understanding of love changed after reading this chapter? How?

4. Do you have a relationship which involves trust as defined in this chapter? Talk about instances in which that trust was put to the test.

5. What have you used in the past to dull the pain of your own loneliness or difficult relationships?

6. Have you ever thought about the possibility for yourself of a relationship with God? Is it hard for you to believe such a relationship can exist? Why or why not?

 Explore the Bible

The Explore the Bible portion of this book invites you to discover for yourself what the Bible says about the issues raised.

If you are not familiar with the Bible, take your time. Use the Contents page to help you. (Scripture passages are printed out for you in this first chapter.) If you have trouble understanding what you are reading, ask a friend to help, or go on to the next reading.

Take time to quietly think about what the passages mean to you. It may help to read the verses that come before or after. If you find yourself resisting what the passage says, simply note that resistance and go on. Try not to give up.

TRUTH

1 Timothy 2:3-4—"God our Savior...wants all [people] to be saved and to come to a knowledge of the truth."

1 John 3:18-19—"Let us not love with words or tongue but with actions and truth. This then is how we know that we belong to the truth, and how we set our hearts at rest in his presence."

Proverbs 12:22—"The Lord detests lying lips, but he delights in [those] who are truthful."

LOVE

1 Corinthians 13:4-7—"Love is patient, love is kind. It does not envy, it does not boast, it is not proud. It is not rude, it is not self-seeking, it is not easily angered, it keeps no record of wrongs. Love does not delight in evil but rejoices with the truth. It always protects, always trusts, always hopes, always perseveres."

TRUST

Psalm 9:10—"Those who know your name will trust in you, for you, Lord, have never forsaken those who seek you."

Proverbs 3:5—"Trust in the Lord with all your heart and lean not on your own understanding; in all your ways acknowledge him, and he will make your paths straight."

Nahum 1:7—"The Lord is good, a refuge in times of trouble. He cares for those who trust in him."

Up Close and Personal

David's prayers

You may have heard of David, the young boy called upon by God and countrymen to defend his people against the giant Goliath. David eventually became the greatest king of Israel. Over the course of his life, he made terrible mistakes and awful things happened to him. Yet over the long haul he was known to have sought a relationship with God with all his heart.

In the book of Psalms, we are privileged to listen in on many of David's prayers—his honest conversations with God. These prayers reflect a wide range of emotions, from anger toward God, to fear for enemies, to total love and trust.

Read Psalm 86.

1. First, look for clues about David's present situation.

2. Next, find specific phrases which speak of:
   a. God's love for David and vice versa;
   b. David's doubts and fears;
   c. David's reasons for trusting God.

3. What evidence do you find in this psalm that David did not find it necessary to guard his words with God? What does this indicate about an intimate relationship with God?

Read Psalm 71. Some think this prayer may have been written when David was an old man and close to death.

1. Find passages that give you clues to David's present situation.

2. What do David's deepest desires seem to be after a lifetime of knowing God?

2

What happened to Paradise?

Frank was a big man, a construction worker with huge, dangerous-looking hands. A passing driver had picked Frank up as he hitchhiked in rural Appalachia after his car had broken down. Now they sat talking over a cup of coffee at a truck stop.

For some reason, Frank poured out his life's story, to the amazement of the driver: Several months before, someone had stolen all of a fellow worker's tools. So Frank took the man to a hardware store and loaned him a thousand dollars—Frank's entire savings—to buy enough tools to continue his work. The next day the "friend" disappeared, along with his promise of repayment. A few weeks later, Frank encountered the man in a bar. Frank dragged him outside and broke all the fingers on his right hand.

As Frank told more of his story, this tough, macho man started to cry. The most traumatic of his memories came from his time in the Army. The soldiers had befriended a small Vietnamese girl. One day the enemy strapped a mine to her back and set her walking toward Frank's camp. He watched her being killed by the blast. The bomb also turned Frank's best buddy into a blind paraplegic.

Frank had never recovered from these memories. Upon his return to the States he found some solace in his marriage to a beautiful girl. But she had just informed Frank she no longer loved him and told him to leave their house. A broken man, he begged the *stranger who sat across the restaurant table from him to answer his questions, "How can people do things like this to each other? Why is our world so full of misery?"*

Frank was asking key questions about the evil in others and, worse still, in himself. He suffered bitter losses that translated themselves into acts of cruel revenge. He didn't like what he had become. His life was anything but happy and fulfilled, and he was desperate to stop the destructive cycle.

We have defined intimacy—the key to peace and happiness—in terms of truth, love, and trust. These are good and desirable things. But what has happened to make intimacy so difficult to find? For the answer, we look to Genesis, the first book of the Bible.

In the first chapters we meet Adam and Eve. God created them as his very own children, sharing every wonderful thing with them. Then God gave them the responsibility and privilege of co-ruling the earth. So Adam and Eve lived in a perfect world, knew perfect love, and had direct, intimate contact with God. This is what life would have—should have—been for us, too. Except, something went wrong.

For the first humans to become truly responsible adults, worthy of the trust God gave them, they had to confront and survive a sort of adolescent crisis of choice. God had not created them as puppets or slaves, but as companions capable of the deepest kind of intimate relationship. God made Adam and Eve capable of freely choosing the love and care available to them as children of a loving father.

Adam and Eve reached a point when they had to choose whether to trust and follow God's values. It was not as if God had given them an extensive rulebook. Set before the couple was only one boundary, one stipulation, which, if honored, would keep the trust among them intact. Tragically, Adam and Eve did not accept God's loving limits on their

God did not create us as puppets or slaves, but as companions capable of the deepest kind of intimate relationship.

behavior. They chose to determine the course of their own lives by crossing the line of God's trust.

In a sense, Adam and Eve stole God's right to put one simple restriction on the relationship, and started creating the rules for the relationship themselves. So they did the one prohibited thing, which was to eat the fruit of the forbidden tree of the knowledge of good and evil.

The consequences span the ages

The impact of their choice has rumbled down through the ages like thunder. When God confronted Adam and Eve about what they had done, they lied. Truth was lost. Shame, fear, and guilt entered the human condition. Not only did they lose their perfect relationship with God, they lost it with each other as well. They accused each other, failing to take responsibility for their own actions.

In acting against God's instructions, the couple demonstrated lack of trust in God's character, and in the boundaries God had created with their well-being in mind. When they realized what they had done, Adam and Eve's first response was to cover their nakedness. This action symbolized the destruction of trust, and the beginning of deceit and self-protection. Now both truth and trust were gone.

Paradise was lost. A world of cooperation became a world of competition. The strong began to oppress and exploit the weak. Human relationships became a battleground instead of a serene garden. As humanity multiplied, social stress was mirrored in the human body as well. Disease now became a possibility, as would death by natural disaster. Aging accelerated. Physical death by some means became inevitable.

The essence of life with God was lost. By inheriting the human condition all of humanity died to the voice of God. We also died to the fullest potential for joy in relationships with other human beings. Indeed, every sphere of human life has been tainted or dominated by the opposites of love, truth, and trust—hate, pride and indifference, lies, and rebellion. Human beings have become dangerous to each other, possessing the potential for evil. Everyone now has a character that is to some degree in opposition to the perfection God created in mankind in the beginning. What a terrible cycle Adam and Eve began!

Spiritual consequences

We cannot know in this life the nature of the direct, spiritual communication Adam and Eve first experienced with God. It remains a mystery. Nor can we imagine perfect and total trust between each other as human beings. We hear about "spiritual" experiences with God, but generally we do not begin to understand what that means. It is as if God originally had created our forebears with a seventh sense. If we now discover we have lost that sense, it means little because we cannot comprehend the thing lost. Does a person blind from birth ever comprehend sight?

God longs to communicate love for us, and to guide us in every aspect of our life. There is no greater intimacy conceivable.

It was God's desire in the beginning that his spirit actually reside within every human being. God longs to communicate love for us from within our very selves, and to guide us in every aspect of our life. There is no greater intimacy conceivable. It would mean spending every waking moment of our lives conscious of our unity and companionship with God. That kind of intimacy is what each of us lost when Adam and Eve made their rebellious choice.

The story doesn't end there

How depressing this all seems. Consider Frank once more. He was a sensitive man. But he had absorbed the hate and violence around him, a legacy from Adam and Eve and their descendants. His experiences of horror saturated his spirit, and he became a bitter, raging man.

Yet there is hope for the Franks of the world—for all of us touched by the bitter disappointments of this life. The evil in our life can lead to spiritual and physical death. But God has a cure, a plan for our eternal happiness. The good news is that the biblical story does not end with Adam and Eve. Their failure is only the beginning.

As we shall see later, God devised a plan for full restoration of spiritual oneness—intimacy with God. The kind of spiritual unity that leads to lasting contentment is available now to those who love God. It is possible for us today to enter into a life of deepening intimacy with God—to listen to and speak with God, to enjoy at least in part the everyday communication Adam and Eve once shared with their father.

Someday, those who accept this plan can be with God completely and permanently. We will no longer need to struggle in our search for intimacy, love, and happiness. But for now, there is a way to be "reconnected"—to be born again spiritually and to know how to live at peace with God and with other people. This is the great promise of Christianity. This is the hope we can share.

Talk It Over

1. Have you had bitter disappointments in your own life? To what extent have the evils of this world hardened you? Why?

2. Would you say, in general, that you are a hopeful person? What is the source of that hope? Is hopelessness like Frank's played out in your home? Your community?

3. Before reading this chapter, how would you have answered Frank's question: "Why is our world so full of misery?"

4. Think about your own "crisis of adolescent choice" (see page 19). Was yours a smooth transition into adulthood, or full of rebellion, like Adam and Eve's? Why?

5. Do your desires prevent you from searching for your spiritual "seventh sense"? (See p. 21.)

 Explore the Bible

As you explore the Bible today, you are asked to look up, read, and consider longer portions of Scripture. Don't worry about understanding every word. Get the general idea.

1. Read Romans 1:20-32. In this passage a great Christian leader named Paul describes how the world got in such a mess. Do you agree with his assessment? Why or why not?

2. Read Psalm 42 and Psalm 56. When King David wrote these poems, he was in big trouble, experiencing depression and persecution. People were even trying to kill him. What words does he use to describe the evils of the world

gathering forces against him? Can you identify with the feelings he expresses? What response to his situation did he choose?

 # Up Close and Personal

Read the Bible's account in Genesis 2:4–3:24 of Adam and Eve's rebellion.

1. Do the details of this story bear any similarities to your own break with your parents?

2. Examine the issues of intimacy—love, truth, and trust—in relation to this Bible story. Exactly how was each lost with God, and between Adam and Eve?

3. Discuss this statement: "After Adam and Eve, human relationships would become a battleground rather than a serene garden. Men's greater physical strength contrasted with women's dependency began the reality of the oppression of the weak by the strong that would mark virtually all human relationships in the future."

4. "It is impossible to live in this world without being tainted by hate, lies, and rebellion at unconscious levels of thinking and feeling. Since Adam and Eve, every human being now possesses a character that is to some extent in opposition to the perfect moral character of God." Do you believe this statement is true? Why or why not?

3

Can't buy me love

Rose was a vivacious, outgoing young woman from a large Irish family. Aspects of her faith had always been satisfying and meaningful. However, while she felt God's presence at Mass and found the rituals comforting, she couldn't seem to bring the feeling home. She simply couldn't get a grip on disturbing aspects of her personality—especially her temper and the guilt that followed her periodic explosions.

For months at a time she would try harder, and feel good about herself. But then she'd lose control again and be back at ground zero. "Be kind to yourself," her much-loved, gentle priest would say. Yet at the end of each day, she reviewed her life ledger with the meticulousness of a bookkeeper, hoping to find more good deeds than bad. When she was pretty sure that the day's ledger was not in her favor, she would wait nervously until Saturday Confession and Sunday Mass to get her account back into the black for Monday morning.

Then a famous Christian evangelist came to town, and she found herself praying at the front of the stadium after the sermon. Rose realized she had found the secret of Kofi, her friend at the office. He seemed so serene, not aggressive or uptight. She had puzzled over his type of Christianity. Now she understood. Her upbringing had emphasized rules, rituals, and obedience grounded in the fear of God. Now she discovered God as a loving heavenly father who wanted her love and respect, but never her fear.

Now, when she occasionally lost her famous temper, she wasn't terrified of losing her soul. Amazingly, however, she wasn't losing control as often or as loudly. Instead of worrying about her temper and feeling guilty, she talked to God throughout the day, and had a special time with him each evening after her kids were in bed. In her relationship with God Rose had found peace and happiness that had begun to keep her violent temper in check.

She also found a church full of people like Kofi who talked openly about how God was helping them in important areas of their lives. Her faith made sense for the first time in her life, and it made a difference in the areas that mattered most.

The search for intimacy is a search for acceptance—with God and other human beings. Rose found herself in such a search, as do we all. But Rose was going about the search with a basic and common misunderstanding: that humans beings can convince God of their fundamental worthiness, and thus gain God's approval by creating a ledger stamped "good enough."

The "religious" solution

Human beings have always sensed that they didn't start out in a right relationship with God. How we get back into a loving, healthy, accepting relationship has occupied the human mind as long as anyone can remember. Human logic concludes that the solution for this problem is to simply buckle down and make sure that we have deposited more good deeds than bad in our "relationship account." If we have not been kind, we are "in the red" and the relationship won't work. If we are doing good, the relationship is "in the

*The search for intimacy is
a search for acceptance—
with God and other
human beings.*

black." So surely if we do enough good works, God is obliged to love us.*

The problems with this approach are many. For example, who defines "naughty" and "nice"? What are the correct criteria for us to meet before we can feel secure in our future? Success? Money? Loving relationships? The number of times we've been to church or given to good causes? Who can say she has always been good in every situation? And how do we explain why bad things happen to good people and vice versa?

But the major problem with this way of thinking is that God is not a greedy banker stamping our accounts "credit" or "overdrawn," or a Santa Claus who only rewards goodness. God is more like a concerned parent—a perfect parent—who loves his children whether they are being good or being bad. If earthly parents can love their children without conditions, surely God, who is love, loves us all the more. God is not pleased or satisfied by our attempts to buy his love with good deeds. How would a truly loving parent feel

---

*This system of thinking has also been used to explain how a person gets to heaven (or not): A person is good, he gets the divine stamp of approval, and goes to heaven. Not good, she goes to hell. Or, if people don't believe in an eternal destination, they at least believe that goodness leads one to prosperity and happiness. Conversely, wrongdoing must lead to personal disaster, loneliness, or poverty.

We all know we cannot buy the love of a human being. Why then would we dare to think we can buy God's love with good deeds or religiosity?

overhearing a child say, "Well, I think I've given Dad enough presents so that he'll love me now"?

Let's look at it another way. Suppose, for the sake of argument, that good deeds could cancel out bad ones. Let's also suppose that several times a month a man becomes violently drunk, abuses his family, spends food money on drink, and risks lives while driving. When sober he would have to enter into a flurry of frenzied good works in an attempt to cancel out all the horrible things done while drunk and to purchase God's favor. Even if, in principle, he could do enough good deeds to cancel out the bad ones, that would still not be adequate to address his patterns of abuse. Clearly, he has to get to the root problem and find a way to change his behavior if he is going to be able to reestablish a relationship of love and intimacy with his wife and children.

If we know we cannot buy the love of a human being, then why would we dare to think we can buy God's love with good deeds or religiosity? Strangely enough, however, most people's mental picture of religion is nothing more than an organized method for performing enough good deeds to earn God's love for eternity. We already have God's love. What we lack is a clear understanding of God's parental concern for our well-being, and the maturity to lead lives that please God out of a reciprocated love for him.

Victimized...or responsible?

We noted in the last chapter that every one of us is characterized by an astonishing capacity for self-deception. Even love itself is often tainted by selfish motivation. However, we resist the idea that we are contaminated with evil because most of us view ourselves as victims of our messed up world, and not part of the problem. Perhaps we feel we were not loved as we should have been by our parents. We have been badly treated by others who were supposed to love us. Our understanding is growing of how painful childhood can be even in loving families. Therefore, we recognize how true it is that virtually all of us are, to some extent, victims of our fallen, hurting world.

If we are honest with ourselves, we will reject this current "culture of victimization" trend, and recognize that in the light of God's absolute moral perfection, we are responsible for much wrongdoing. Each of us has our own victims, usually those we claim to love. We disobeyed and lied to our parents. We are too busy to spend time with our own children. We say devastating things to our spouse, knowing the point of greatest vulnerability at which to plunge in our knife of sarcasm. This ability to selfishly hurt those we love is one of the important aspects of what the Bible calls sin: actions or attitudes totally incompatible with the character of God.*

Acknowledging our own responsibility is a key step toward intimacy with God. Only when we take this step can we view ourselves honestly, seeing ourselves the way God sees us. Only then can we draw closer to finding out what our future will be like and who we will become if we step into a relationship with God. In order to know these answers,

---

*"Sins" are never lists of "fun" things that God arbitrarily decides to call bad. Sins are actions and attitudes that separate us from other people or God. Sin "disconnects" because it makes us spiritually incompatible with what is good or healthy in God, others, or even ourselves.

we must also have a true and accurate understanding of God. Who is God, the other person in the relationship? If we perceive God as the one who holds our eternal destiny, then how will this person handle the question of our behavior?

God's character

Most people have a distorted view of God. On the one hand, they may believe God is only loving, kind, and totally forgiving, overlooking all human wrong. Is it really necessary, people ask, to think that God would discriminate against those who, for some reason, are unable and unwilling to believe in him? How could a loving God send anyone to eternal punishment?

On the other hand, some people view God as the stern judge who can see us only as vile and repugnant compared to his own perfection. This God seems to take pleasure in dangling us above the fire while laughing at our vulnerability to his fickle will.

Both of these are distorted views of God, holding only a small measure of truth. On the one hand, God *is* totally loving. On the other hand, God *is* morally perfect and must be the administrator of justice.

Sometimes the demands of love and justice seem to be in conflict. Imagine being a Jew during the Nazi holocaust, or perhaps the parents of a child killed by a terrorist bomb.

God's loving justice meant giving us what we needed, not what we deserved.

Would you feel loved by a God who simply forgave the perpetrators of those crimes when they hadn't even admitted that they had done anything wrong? For a victim, doesn't loving justice mean requiring condemnation for the one who hurt him?

Or imagine that your father is a famous judge noted for his justice. Now suppose you had been caught speeding at well over 100 miles per hour while intoxicated. When you are brought before your father the judge, should he pronounce you not guilty because you are his son or daughter? Would he still be a just judge if he did?

If we are honest, we have to admit that we don't really want a God of justice at all. We want a God who will inflict punishment on those who hurt us, and overlook it when we hurt others. This a perfect God cannot do. So, God needed to find a way of dealing with our sins and wrongdoings. True to his character, God's response to this predicament was both loving and just.

The human solution—hoping that good deeds can outweigh our bad deeds—not only makes a mockery of intimacy, it mocks God's justice as well. The human solution implies that God cares more about our performance than our character. In reality, God's plan involved more than simplistic ideas of punishment. God wanted to change people from the inside, and to give us the power and the means to live within the boundaries for safety that he creates. He didn't simply want to take away the guilt of our sin; he wanted to deal with our tendency to sin and loose us from the power and penalty of sin. God's loving justice meant giving us what we needed, not what we deserved. All this he did because he loves us.

Rose's temper had been a block to intimacy with God and with people she dearly loved. God took her temper very seriously. As Rose found out, God's solution to her problem demonstrates both perfect love and perfect justice. God's plan took away her guilt from the past while helping her deal with the present. Rose discovered that God deals with problems such as hers without compromising his own perfection and without seeming to say that the evil in our lives doesn't really matter.

As a loving parent, God's overwhelming desire is for what the Bible calls "reconciliation"—the restoration of relationship. Like Rose, none of us can possibly buy a healthy relationship with God with any amount of good deeds. Nor can we solve our sin problems by ourself, even if we recognize our responsibility to do so. As we will see in the next chapter, God alone had the solution—one of breathtaking creativity, and unspeakable sacrifice.

 **Talk It Over**

1. Think back over your actions the past week. Can you identify a list of bad deeds and good deeds? How do the good deeds make you feel? How do the bad things make you feel?

2. What is your predominant characteristic that causes you and others problems? How do you feel about it? Are you able to claim responsibility for the consequences of your actions? Or are they usually someone else's fault?

3. What do you think about heaven and hell? Do you recall how your beliefs developed?

4. Discuss the example on page 30 of the child killed by a terrorist bomb. Suppose you had planted the bomb. What do you think God's response should be? What would your response be if you were the judge?

Explore the Bible

A true picture of God is key to understanding Christianity. Since the entire Bible is in essence a description of God, you cannot possibly get a complete picture in a few minutes of Bible search. However, you can begin by looking up the following verses (try 2-3 a day if the list seems long). What descriptive words about God are found in each passage? Suggested answers are printed on page 34.

1. Jeremiah 32:27
2. 2 Chronicles 30:9
3. Nehemiah 9:17
4. Job 34:10-12
5. Psalm 47:7
6. Psalm 68:6
7. Luke 5:21
8. Romans 2:11
9. 1 John 4:8, 16

 # Up Close and Personal

Read Luke 18:9-14

In this passage Jesus compares two very different attitudes toward a relationship with God. It is helpful to know that the Pharisee was a member of a Jewish religious group that prided themselves on trying to keep the very tiniest details of what they thought were God's requirements. A tax collector, on the other hand, was as vile an enemy as a Pharisee could imagine, for a tax collector worked for the

Roman government which was occupying the Jews' homeland. If being a traitor to your own people wasn't bad enough, tax collectors made their living by charging more than the Romans required and pocketing the difference.

1. How would you characterize the attitude these two men brought to their prayers to God?

2. One man had dedicated his life to obedience to God, the other to the conscious betrayal of God's people. How could Jesus think God is more pleased with the one man than the other?

3. Does this story imply that God prefers people who are consciously bad to those who consciously attempt to please him? Why or why not?

4. Why would God value an attitude of the heart more than conformity to the legal requirements of the Jewish religion, that he himself commanded?

5. How does this story give you more or less hope as you think about the possibility of a relationship with God?

6. How does one cultivate an attitude like that of the tax collector while living a life more like that of the Pharisee? Is it possible?

Possible answers for Explore the Bible

1. *the Lord; all-powerful*
2. *gracious, compassionate*
3. *forgiving, slow to anger*
4. *cannot do wrong, be unjust*
5. *ruler of all the earth*
6. *sets the lonely in families*
7. *forgiver of sins*
8. *shows no favoritism*
9. *love*

4

God moves first

Barry and Dale were inseparable friends in high school, Barry the center and Dale the quarterback of the championship football team. Both grew up on farms and loved tinkering with old cars. From the moment they met in second grade, they enjoyed an unusual bond.

Later, in college, they shared an apartment and the friendship grew even deeper—until one afternoon Barry found his fiancée in a deep, passionate embrace with another man. The man was Dale. Barry lost his best friend and fiancée in one terrible moment.

Dale's relationship with Barry's ex-fiancée didn't last. He too had lost his best friend, and now a woman he'd thought he loved. He missed Barry, but he knew there was no way Barry could ever forget his betrayal.

Barbara and Jennifer were deepest friends. From the moment they met in their professional office, they shared a bond of mutual appreciation and trust. Together they rejoiced in both daily tasks and life's major passages. Then the unspeakable happened. Jennifer betrayed a trust, divulging a secret failure of Barbara's to a casual acquaintance.

Barbara, totally shaken, withdrew into bottomless depression. That others would know of her secret guilt drove her into seclusion. She was unable to function at the office, and eventually quit her job. When she finally was able to cope with life again, she found it hard to trust or befriend anyone. She had lost her career, her income, her confidence, and her best friend.

Jennifer suffered too. Only vaguely did she understand why her betrayal was so devastating to Barbara. Not understanding Barbara's coldness, Jennifer also backed away. Was what she did so terrible, she reasoned? Trying to find other friends, she resumed life the best she could.

The problem with broken relationships is that rarely will one or the other person make the first move toward reconciliation. It is only reasonable that the person at fault must make the first move. Of course, it is always the other person's fault....

The obvious requirement for reconciliation is that at least one party relinquish the need to "win," the right to hold out for recognition of the wrong and the request for forgiveness. Oftentimes the cause of the breach is not a trivial lack of consideration, but utter betrayal that has cost the betrayed virtually everything of value. Then, it would seem, there is no hope. Few people seem strong enough to suffer a wrong and be the one to offer forgiveness first, thereby initiating the reconciliation and a second chance.

The Bible describes just this kind of stalemate between us and God. Humanity seemed incapable of making any move toward God because of attitudes of rebellion and an immense capacity for self-deception. Some people feel secure and in charge only when they are stubbornly trying to subordinate others' wills—even God's—to their own. Throughout all time, people's relationships with God and others have degenerated into battlefields of pride on which the rules of engagement are manipulation, domination, and control.

The Bible makes it clear—mankind, not God, is responsible for the rift between humanity and God. We have spoiled the image of God in which we were created. We have reduced the perfect home God gave us to moral, social, and ecological chaos. The first move should be ours. Yet

The problem with broken relationships is that rarely will one or the other person make the first move.

from within the rubble of a ruined world, we dare to shake our fist in God's face, or to run from God in humiliation.

God's daring strategy

From within a heart of perfect love, strength, wisdom, and compassion, God thought the unthinkable: God would make the first move. The plan is brilliant. God, the all-powerful ruler of the universe would re-form himself into a human being, coming to Earth, no less, as a baby. After thirty-three years he would subordinate himself to a world which hated him, to the extent of allowing them to kill him in one of the most barbaric forms of execution ever invented. Why? So that the score could be settled, the reconciliation completed and intimate friendship restored once again.

The key player in this drama is Jesus, God's only son. The only requirement from human beings is that we do God the simple courtesy of treating his plan seriously, acknowledging the perfectly obvious fact that God's plan is our only hope.

Jesus, God in the flesh

The Bible tells us much about Jesus' miraculous birth, but very little about his childhood. He was a carpenter's adopted son, the child of a godly mother. When Jesus started his public ministry as a teacher at about age thirty, he was at first a folk hero. Traveling extensively, he spoke about issues close to God's heart. He demonstrated power over nature, disease, and hostile supernatural forces. Not surprisingly, he became a celebrity and thousands flocked to hear and see him.

In the midst of this growing popularity, Jesus set about building a group of devoted, teachable followers, a small community of friends among whom real love could be shared. He offered healing to the outcasts of society by treating them as persons worthy of his, and thus their own, respect. He offered them the possibility of a relationship with God. He also offered them the potential for human intimacy, because the extent to which people are loved without conditions has a great influence on their ability both to receive and to offer intimacy.

In his physical life on earth Jesus showed us that it is possible to live a spiritually healthy and completely holy life. He set the standard for moral character. In Jesus' words and actions, he also showed us God's mind and heart, what God thinks and cares about.

Yet, as important as all this was to God's plan to restore his relationship with humanity, it was far from sufficient. If Jesus had only lived and died a good teacher, he still would not have restored our relationship with God, nor changed us and enabled us to have a character like that of God. For this to be achieved Jesus had to take onto himself the full consequences of humanity's refusal to reconcile with God. That required both physical punishment, and temporary separation from God the Father.

Jesus' death

You may have heard the story of how God took the initiative. Through a series of events, prepared in eternity, all the guilt of sin from all of human history came to rest on Jesus when he suffered and died on the cross. God took all the punishment that should have been given to each individual and laid it on Jesus instead. God's own selfless, totally innocent son willingly accepted the ultimate pain and punishment in our place.

From within a heart of perfect love, strength, wisdom, and compassion, God thought the unthinkable: God would make the first move.

How could God be just and allow an innocent person to suffer and die for everyone else? What about this was fair? It could only happen if that individual was God himself.

When we experience the pain, brokenness, and loneliness that comes from living in a wicked world, we must remember that God has experienced that pain, only multiplied infinitely. This is a wonderful and comforting thought, but at this point in our story it would appear that evil conquered God. God could now forgive us, overlooking our sin, which he transferred onto Jesus. But Jesus actually *died*. The crucifixion appeared to be the final chapter.

Jesus' death is *not* the end

Thankfully, the story is not finished. Jesus experienced the full measure of alienation from God the Father for three days. His body was dead, but his spirit lived on. The separation, however, was not to last. On the day Christians now celebrate as Easter, Jesus was restored to his body and reunited with God's eternal Spirit. Jesus walked again among his disciples. He touched them and they touched him. He ate and talked with them, then one day returned to heaven, his mission completed. From there he would send the Holy Spirit, the very Spirit of God, to live within each person who loves him and who is prepared to commit to a trusting relationship with him.

*How could God be just and
allow an innocent person to die?
It could only happen if that
individual was God himself.*

Barry and Dale, and Jennifer and Barbara experienced only a small taste of the agony of separation God felt when he sent Jesus to die. Jesus' death was, for God, as bad as a mother or father watching an only son tortured and murdered before their very eyes. We must remember how costly all this was to God. From this realization grows the love Christians have toward God. When a friend takes the step of reconciliation toward us when we don't deserve it, we feel only a small portion of the gratitude we extend to God for his gracious act through Jesus Christ.

Because God was willing to take this first step, every human being can know that the pain we bear, physical or otherwise, was experienced in far greater measure by God himself in the person of Jesus Christ. Also, we can know that separations caused by sin or error need have only a temporary influence on us. Jesus fully understands betrayal and how hard it is to forgive. Therefore, he knows what he is doing when he says we also should forgive.

God so desired a relationship with you and me that he took the first step of reconciliation. In no way did we deserve what God did; we were the offenders. This is courageous love, which, if we follow God's example in its practice, can make all the difference in the world in our earthly relationships also, and in an eternally wonderful life with God.

Talk It Over

1. Have you ever experienced a broken relationship? How did it feel? How did the situation affect you?

2. Have you ever tried to selflessly offer forgiveness to a person who would not accept it? What motivated you? How did it turn out?

3. What kind of person do you visualize Jesus to be in view of his actions? Some people find it hard to believe that Jesus could have been perfect. What movies have you seen, or other media events, that show Jesus in a less than ideal or perfect light? What is a perfect person like?

4. People often think that Jesus was murdered. While this is true, the Bible says that God oversaw Jesus' death in such a way that the plan of salvation and reconciliation could be accomplished. Is this a new thought to you? What does it tell you about God?

Explore the Bible

1. Fill in the missing words to get a picture of God's plan of reconciliation with mankind (use an NIV Bible if possible):

   a. Romans 8:7: "The sinful mind is _____ to God."

   b. Colossians 1:21: "Once you were _____ from God and were enemies in your minds because of your evil behavior."

   c. Colossians 1:19-20: "God was pleased to have all his fullness dwell in [Christ], and through him to reconcile to himself all things...by making _____ through his blood, shed on the cross."

2. Now read Ephesians 2:11-22. This passage refers to two groups—Jews and Gentiles—in those days who were about as alienated as people can be. What does the writer of Ephesians claim that God accomplished through the cross? How does that apply to us today—to our relationships? To the entire world?

 ## Up Close and Personal

A New Testament story dealing with betrayal, guilt, humiliation, forgiveness, and reconciliation is found in John 13:36-38; 18:1-17; and 21:1-17. Peter's denial of knowing Jesus after being his intimate friend for several years is a captivating story laced into the entire account of Jesus' death and resurrection. It is in itself a mini-picture of the entire salvation story: how God, so betrayed, could act in such love.

Try also to read the entire account of the crucifixion in the book of John this week. Which characters in the story do you relate to the most?

—Pilate (one in authority with a big decision to make);

—The disciples (close to Jesus, afraid to act);

—The crowd (making false claims leading to the discrediting of Jesus);

—The soldiers (carrying out their orders in taunting and crucifying Jesus)

—Others....

5

The life-changing choice

On the surface, Aubrey appeared to be one of the most generous, skilled, and trustworthy persons anyone could ever meet. He cared for an 85-year-old man in a neighboring apartment who grew progressively more ill and senile and eventually died. Aubrey cooked a meal for him every day, cleaned, and even took care of his banking. Everyone in Aubrey's apartment complex knew he would be willing to help them if they were ever in need.

Aubrey was a good man. But he was not very good at handling what was becoming the wreck of his own life. Aubrey was a drug addict. As a well-dressed professional, his income selling medical supplies more than covered the cost of his lifestyle and his habit. But inwardly, Aubrey was wasting away—physically and spiritually.

Aubrey knew he had secret needs. Once he attended a Promise Keepers rally with a friend from work. He even started going to a Bible study. In a moment of honesty, he told some Christian friends about his addiction. They urged him to stop, which he did for a while. But later he explained that he really didn't want or need to stop. He argued it was a financial issue more than a moral or *health issue. Drugs were simply how he relaxed, and were clearly giving him an edge in his job. With higher commissions coming in, he could afford the habit. Why, he asked, should Christians tell him this was some sort of sin?*

Aubrey still believes he seeks God. But he cannot imagine going through life without the wonderful feeling he gets from his drugs. Aubrey wants to negotiate with God; he wants both a relationship with God and his self-destructive lifestyle. But can he keep on like this, ignoring God's clear directions when it comes to important decisions?

Many people have lifestyles that they know God cannot approve of. Some even mistakenly think it courageous to risk hoping that God will accept them anyway. These misconceptions and self-delusions are keeping them from experiencing the joy of life with God. God puts limits on our behavior because he loves us. If Aubrey truly wants an intimate relationship with God, he will need to come to the point of allowing God to set those limits for his own good. So do we all.

Looking back at the previous chapters, let's review what we now know about coming into relationship with God. So far we have seen that, according to the Bible and confirmed by our experiences, each of us has contributed by our own wrongdoing to a world of pain and chaos. We have found that mankind's solution of chalking up good deeds on life's ledger is not enough to bring us happiness here on earth or eternal divine approval. It was God's just and loving solution to send his son Jesus to die for the sins of every person. By acknowledging responsibility for our own sins, and accepting Jesus's death and resurrection on our behalf, we can return to sharing eternal life with our Creator God.

It is time now to seriously consider whether you are prepared to accept God's plan. God, in his gracious patience, will not pry your fingers from your grip on your own des-

The Spirit of Jesus Christ is available to us every moment, not only helping us know what to do, but giving us supernatural power to do it!

tiny. God will not make you believe in Jesus or accept the free gift of deliverance from your life of sin. Unless you at some point make a decision to commit your life to God's way, your relationship with God remains eternally broken.

This is not to say you are a horrible person. Aubrey was far from totally bad. And saying your relationship with God is broken does not imply you are unacquainted with God. You may have talked to God in times of trouble. You may know Bible stories from your childhood in Sunday school. However, mere acquaintance with God does not bring you any of the benefits of Christ's death. If at some point you do not take responsibility for your own sin, you will be continuing to reject God. You will be clinging to the evil in your life, and to the evil of our world. No decision amounts to a decision of "no."

The results of forgiveness

What will happen if you sincerely admit to God your need to be forgiven, and ask God, through Christ, to come change your life? The answer to this question could alleviate some of the reservations you may have about taking the simple but life-changing step of faith necessary to gain eternal peace with God.

First, God's Spirit will come to live inside of you, making it possible for you to change. How many times have you tried to learn a new skill and found yourself making the same mistake over and over again? Perhaps it is learning to serve a tennis ball. A tennis pro could describe to you the correct way to do it. But how wonderful it would be simply to take his skill and plug it into your brain and muscles, to have his voice internally coaching you and his experience guiding your every motion.

This is precisely what God wants to do for each of us. God sends the Spirit of Jesus—the person who lived a perfect life—into the heart and mind of each one who loves him. The Spirit of Jesus Christ is available to Christians every moment, not only helping us know what to do, but giving us supernatural power to do it!

Second, we will acquire a new family, a group of people journeying together in life with the purpose of learning how to be more like Christ. Just as joy, challenge, and sometimes pain are part of human families, God uses the church—the Christian's earthly family—to create situations through which we can grow and change for the better. In this new family, you can be loved and cared for, while practicing the skills of intimacy—love, truth, and trust.

Moreover, within this new worldwide family we are re-formed into the "body of Christ"—Jesus' hands and feet, mouth and heart—to be a team of ambassadors going about doing what Jesus did with supernatural effectiveness while living among humanity. It is a family which values love and justice, and which is committed to spreading the good news of God's plan of reconciliation to every person on earth.

Third, God's ultimate goal is to reconstitute the perfect family he envisioned when he created the ideal world back in the times described in Genesis. The Church is not perfect yet, but will be so at the end of time. God someday will bring history to a close, rid the universe of evil, and re-create Earth to be a home fit once again for God's children.

Christians are the heirs of this promise. They will have lived in this present world and made the choice to be rescued from destruction by trusting Jesus Christ. They will have seen evil and chosen to be good. They will have participated in the battle against wickedness and shared in God's victory over the ultimate evil, death. Through Christ's death on their behalf, the presence of the Holy Spirit, and the ministry of the Body of Christ (the Church) they will be God's new creations, worthy of the title Children of God. They will be co-rulers in the new kingdom God will establish.

The benefits reviewed

So these are the benefits of accepting Christ's death and resurrection on our behalf: (1) freedom from the guilt which separates us from God; (2) the comforting presence of the Spirit of Christ within us to empower and equip us for life; (3) the privilege of participating with a supernaturally guided team of ministers—the Church—who help us to be more like Christ in love and service; and (4) companionship with the eternal family of God as together we co-rule a new heaven and new earth.

Sadly, Aubrey's fear of the unknown and his pride caused him to decide against stopping his destructive habits. He chose temporary comfort through his addiction rather than permanent comfort and joy as one of God's children. The promises of relationship with God, of salvation and freedom from guilt, of a healthier body and spirit, remained for him only ideas. Feeling unwilling and unable to change, Aubrey deprived himself of the wonder and reality of life with God.

What will you do, faced with this life-changing choice?

Talk It Over

1. Like Aubrey, what fears, reservations, or excuses might be keeping you from accepting God's plan of forgiveness, salvation, and reconciliation right now?

2. Is there anything at all about God or this plan which you do not understand?

3. Are you tired of living without the benefits and privileges of being a Christian? Which ones listed in this chapter would you especially like to have present in your life?

 Explore the Bible

1. Read 1 Corinthians 15:3-8, 12-26 (a discussion by Paul of the resurrection); and Acts 2:22-36 (Peter's eyewitness account). Make a list of any ideas in either passage with which you are struggling and why.

2. What do you learn about forgiveness from the following passages?

     —Hebrews 9:22   —Ephesians 1:7

     —1 John 1:9   —Ephesians 4:32

 Up Close and Personal

Read Luke 18:18-25

In this story Jesus confronts a wealthy, deeply religious young man with what would seem to be a most unreasonable request. Elsewhere in the stories of Jesus in the New Testament, Jesus reacts with great kindness to obvious sinners like prostitutes and social outcasts. Generally, he welcomed with gentleness genuine seekers. Nowhere else did he require giving away of all possessions.

1. Why might Jesus be reacting so differently to this young man?

2. Might Jesus' request of this young man have been for his benefit? How?

3. If you were asking Christ how you might have a relationship with him, what aspect of your life might he say has a stronger grip on you than you have on it? Would you be prepared to reprioritize that aspect of your life to establish a relationship of intimacy with God?

4. Why might it be significant that this story directly follows Jesus' description of faith in terms of childlikeness?

6

Ready for new life?

Dave believed it was not bad motives that led to his choice of a seat on the bus next to a young adult woman. In her simple but attractive dress she stood out from the rest of the passengers like a Rolex in a Timex display. Within minutes he found out why he had missed his train and had to take a bus. God wanted her to have a pastor. She was dressed up because she would arrive in Ohio just in time for the funeral of her best friend.

Sarah asked Dave what he did for a living. The pastor told her he was starting a church. "What kind?" she asked. For some reason he gave an answer he had never used before: "I'm trying to start a church that is like a big A.A. meeting, one where people can feel free to say, 'My name is _____ , and I am a _____,' and be honest about the deepest problems in their lives...a big church family where real people can admit to pain and seemingly overwhelming difficulty, be loved just for who they are, and yet be transformed into healthy, functional, and godly persons."

Sarah gave the pastor a strange look. She reached into her bag and pulled out the big blue book that is the "Bible" of Alcoholics Anonymous. Not yet twenty-one, she had been a recovering alcoholic for three years. "You have no idea how much I would like to belong to a church like that," she said.

Perhaps after studying this book you are ready, like Sarah, to say, "Yes, I want what Christianity claims to offer me." The particulars of your life may be much less dire than some of the people described in this book; they may be worse. But in spiritual matters, you realize you need a change. Now you know God's plan of reconciliation, yet you ask, "I'm ready, but how do I begin?"

A new start in life involves at least five steps: (1) recognizing God's love and God's desire to be in a personal relationship with you, (2) confession and repentance, (3) belief in Jesus, (4) counting the cost, and (5) a conscious decision to ask Jesus to come into your life and take charge. We have already talked about step one. Let's examine the others.

Confess and repent

The word *confess* in the Bible means "to agree with." God has a radically different view of us than we do. We have discussed at length that we caused God the pain of separation, hurting ourselves and others as well. Coming to God means acknowledging our guilt, *agreeing with* God about it. Think about this irony. In the heavenly court of justice, Jesus—who took our guilt upon himself—can declare us innocent only if we first declare ourselves guilty. In essence we align our view of ourselves with that of God. This is called confession.

In the heavenly court of justice, Jesus—who took our guilt upon himself—can declare us innocent only if we first declare ourselves guilty.

However, confession is not quite enough. We have to repent. The meaning of repentance in the original language of the New Testament is "to turn around and go in the opposite direction." We stop going our own way and turn back to God. We make a U-turn. While confession is a recognition in our minds that we have done something wrong, repentance reflects a genuine desire not to do that wrong again. It is an act of the will to decide that, with God's power and help at our disposal, we will be actively choosing not to sin again.

The major error we need to confess is that we have gone our own way without God. But included in that general recognition of our waywardness are numerous changes of direction to make, or sins to abandon. First consider whether or not you are ready to share your life with God. If so, then ask God to show you some specific aspects of life where your behavior and attitudes stand in the way of a meaningful relationship with him. Which selfish qualities that destroy intimacy does God want you to confess and repent of?

Most people have habits and attitudes they know they will have to change immediately. But as we go along in our new Christian life, God gradually reveals other actions we need to deal with. You don't have to worry about examining every detail of your life right away. Part of God's plan is a gradual unfolding of his desires for us.

Believe in Jesus

"Believing" is an exercise of the mind. Intellectual agreement with the facts about Jesus is an aspect of faith which we dare not minimize. It is fashionable to believe that Jesus is one way of many possible ways to find God, and that sincere belief in any religion is equally as effective. But notice the basics of other religions. They are codes of conduct set out by human beings most of whom are now dead. Christianity is the only religion which offers a *relationship* with a *living* God.

Knowing Jesus is the only true way to know God. He came to Earth as a human being, both fully divine and fully

*Christianity is the only religion which offers a **relationship** with a **living** God.*

human. He died and physically rose from the dead, returning to heaven to rule the universe as a living person. Either you believe these facts, or you reject Jesus. Jesus is not only a great teacher. Jesus claimed to be God. Therefore, either Jesus was a fraud and an insane liar, or he is The Truth. Assess the person of Jesus as described in the Bible. Then either believe in him as God and Savior, or don't. There is no middle ground.

The key is to combine intellectual agreement with the facts about Jesus with a demonstration of that belief in action. Belief within an intimate, vital relationship is called trust. It is possible, let's say, to believe without a doubt that a certain person is of impeccable character, attractive, and available. It is another thing altogether to say "I do" to a set of questions that binds you to him or her for life, to the exclusion of all others. Or it is one thing to believe that an ice skating partner will catch you in perfect safety after a high triple jump. It is another thing altogether to actually make the jump. In each case, we can draw a distinction between "belief about" and "belief in." Trusting Jesus means exerting your will to be in relationship with him daily, even in potentially dangerous situations.

Count the cost

Any belief that involves intimacy with another person also requires commitment. It is costly to have a best friend, a spouse, a child. But rarely can we foresee the entire cost when we enter the relationship. Some of these relationships end precisely because we did not adequately consider the cost.

Let's face it, we live in a society which downplays commitment. "I'll promise to *try* to love you through sickness and health, but if I'm not up to it, I'll quit." Or, "I'll say I'll show up at this project or that, but if something more entertaining comes along, I'll feel free to do that instead." We perceive ourselves as having a right to a perfect life, or perfectly satisfying relationships. So we carefully leave escape clauses or mental reservations in commitments that we entered into as supposedly binding. Counting the cost means intentionally sticking to one's commitment to be loving, truthful, and trusting of God despite anything.

Satan, the spiritual enemy who tempted the first human beings into rebellion, has not given up his futile attempt to destroy God's plan for humanity. Since the resurrection of Jesus from the dead, there is no doubt as to the final outcome of the battle between God and Satan. But Satan is attempting to enslave and destroy as many lives as he can before his ultimate defeat. Satan's main tactic is to implant doubt, uncertainty, and rebelliousness in the minds of Christians, and lure them from a close relationship with God.

Satan also delights in the presence of evil in the world. To be part of the family of God is to join a war against evil. All wars are costly, creating casualties. But Jesus promises a life with potential for overflowing joy and peace, even in the midst of spiritual battle. In some parts of the world, to believe in Jesus is to risk death. In any part of the world, belief in Jesus will involve costly stands against injustice and evil.

You may come to Jesus hurting so badly that all you want and need for a considerable time is to sense the love of God within his family. But as you consider the cost of sharing your life with God, remember that a life with a mission is the only life worth living. God has done a job for you. God will soon have a job for you to do for him.

Are you ready?

Marriage is the one event in human experience which has traditionally signified the deepest and most permanent of commitments. No matter how much prior discussion, assessment of character, and counting of the cost of that relationship over a lifetime, there comes a time when a decision and a promise are made, never to be broken. There is a wedding, a saying of vows, and a declaration of oneness forever between husband and wife.

Similarly, our journey toward a relationship with God has a destination which, like a wedding, also is a beginning. Remember, in the relationship between God and you, God is the pursuer, always asking, "Will you have me?" God has gone to great lengths to bring you to the point where you are considering committing to a relationship with him, his son, and his family, the church. You must now make a decision. Will you confess and repent, believe in Jesus, count the cost and, having done all those things, invite Jesus into your life?

If you wish to have a relationship with God, you need only to proceed as you would with any person: Have a conversation. It's called prayer. Here is a sample of one prayer which you could pray to invite God to be with you throughout the rest of eternity.

Lord Jesus Christ,

I come to you now, knowing that I need to change. Without your help I cannot do this.

I accept that I have betrayed and hurt you. I want to say that I am sorry for (add your own specifics). With your help I intend not to do these things again. Please forgive me for these, and any other sins of which I am not now aware.

Give me the presence and power of your Holy Spirit so that I can become the person you created me to be. Keep showing me how I need to change and give me both the desire and the power to do it.

I accept that there is nothing I have done to deserve forgiveness. But I rely only on what you have done for me. Thank you so much for your life, death, and resurrection on my behalf. Help me, out of gratitude for you, to lead a life from now on that is pleasing to you. Amen.

Reflect for a moment on your thoughts and feelings as you began this study. Who were you then? Now, think about yourself, beginning your *life with God!* Welcome to a new family! It's really this easy.

Remember the kind of church Sarah wanted—a big family where real people could admit to pain and seemingly overwhelming difficulty, be loved just for who they are, and yet be transformed into healthy, functional, and godly persons?

Be aware that every member of your new Christian family started out the same way you did, with the simple realization that they desired a relationship with their creator. Through repentance, confession, and forgiveness, they too began new life.

Like your new brothers and sisters, you now can experience the power given to Christians by the presence of the Holy Spirit in your heart. Like them, you will no longer want to tolerate suffering and injustice when you can work to defeat it. You will both receive love and desire to give it. Regardless of how you or they began their journey in this life, you are all now one family, united by the power of God.

Talk It Over

1. If you prayed the prayer in this chapter, what thoughts and feelings are you experiencing now? Share them. Make your entry into your new life known somehow.

2. Discuss with a Christian friend or a pastor what your next steps should be.

3. If you were helped by this booklet, you may want to consider continuing with the next in the series: *Life With God: Basics for New Christians* from the same publisher.

 # Explore the Bible

Listed here are four key Bible passages which illustrate that being Christian involves head, heart, and action. After studying them, list some specific ways you could demonstrate them in action.

Doing this...	leads to this
Matthew 7:15-23 *Confession*	
James 2:14-17 *Belief*	
1 John 3:11-18 *Love*	
Galatians 6:7-10 *Commitment*	

Up Close and Personal

To understand these stories it is important to know that Zacchaeus was despised by the Jews for being a traitor to his people, and that the Samaritans were viewed as half-breed Jews who had watered down the Jewish faith and built a rival temple to the Jewish temple in Jerusalem. Samaritans were hated by the Jews. Moreover, proper Jewish men never talked to a woman in public, let alone a Samaritan woman, and a loose woman at that. By simply talking to her, Jesus was offering her a respect and dignity she would never have expected from a Jewish man.

Read Luke 19:1-10—the story of Zacchaeus

1. What would have been the personal significance to Zacchaeus of a prominent Jewish celebrity publicly singling him out for the honor of hosting him in his home?

2. What was Zacchaeus's immediate reaction to his being recognized and offered respect by Jesus?

3. Is there any evidence that Jesus required this demonstration of generosity prior to his extension to Zacchaeus of this expression of friendship?

4. What does Zacchaeus's response suggest is the most natural reaction to the discovery that a perfectly holy God loves us so much that he wants to get to know and spend time with us?

Read John 4:1-30—the story of the woman at the well

1. The woman finds out Jesus had always known exactly who and what she was. Therefore, why would Jesus' kindness be so significant to her? Why does she sound happy to announce that he had told her everything about her?

2. What was her response to her discovery of Jesus? What does this suggest is another natural response to our discovery of Jesus' love for us?

3. Why would Jesus have had to bring up the most awkward aspects of this woman's situation? Why do you think he always goes for our most sensitive area when he begins to work with us?

4. If you could have Jesus' love without his confronting your secret or shameful areas, or have his love with the knowledge that he knows about those areas, which would be more valuable to you?

Healing our broken relationship with God

This is an expansion on the information found in chapter 6 on how to step into a relationship with God.

STEP 1: ACKNOWLEDGE THAT YOU REALIZE HOW MUCH GOD LOVES YOU.

STEP 2: SAY "SORRY" TO GOD; DECIDE TO CHANGE

A. Agree with God that you have:

- tried to set your own rules and not accepted God's natural right to have a say in your life.

- run from and been rebellious with God in attitudes and behavior.

- hurt people whom you love even if you didn't mean to.

- lied to yourself about your own goodness.

B. Say "sorry" to God for specific wrongdoing that God brings to mind.

- If you can't think of anything right away, simply ask God to show you areas in your life to be concerned about.

C. Ask God to help you change wrong attitudes and behavior.

- You cannot change on your own; you need God's help but

- God cannot help you until you decide you want to change.

STEP 3: BELIEVE IN JESUS

A. Accept the Bible's claim that the only way to know God is through Jesus Christ.

B. Believe that Jesus is God, that he died and came back to life to heal your broken relationship with God.

C. Reject any other plan for having a relationship with God, including trying to earn God's love by good behavior.

STEP 4: COUNT THE COST

A. Are you willing to put God's purpose and plans for your life ahead of your own goals and desires?

B. Are you ready to face opposition and ridicule from those who do not support your new commitment to God?

C. Are you willing to commit yourself to God's family by becoming part of a local church?

D. Will you join with your new family in telling others about Jesus and in standing for truth and justice at whatever cost?

STEP 5: INVITE JESUS INTO YOUR LIFE

You can do this by saying the following prayer:

Lord Jesus Christ,

I come to you now, knowing that I need to change and that without your help I cannot do this.

I accept that I have upset you and I want to say sorry for (be specific).

Give me the power of the Holy Spirit so I can become the person you made me to be.

Keep showing me how I need to change and give me the desire to do it.

I accept that I can do nothing to deserve your for-giveness. I rely totally on what you have done.

Accept me, forgive me, restore me, and give me good things to do with my life.

Thank you for making me part of your family. Amen.

Notes

Notes

Notes